French Interference in Mexico.

SPEECH

OF

HON. J. A. McDOUGALL,

Of California

IN THE

SENATE OF THE UNITED STATES,

On Tuesday, February 3d, 1863.

BALTIMORE... PRINTED BY JOHN MURPHY & Co.
PUBLISHERS, BOOKSELLERS, PRINTERS AND STATIONERS,
MARBLE BUILDING, 182 BALTIMORE STREET.
1863.

SPEECH.

The Senate having under consideration the resolutions submitted by Mr. McDougall, on the 19th of January last, concerning our relations with France and Mexico—

Mr. McDOUGALL said:

Mr. President: I should have preferred to have had the resolutions to which I now call the attention of the Senate presented by some older Senator than myself, and particularly by some Senator whose relation to the Administration at present in authority would have secured to the subject of the resolutions a more general and careful consideration. I have, however, been compelled to think that gentlemen have purposely and persistently shut their eyes to the position France has assumed, not only towards Mexico, but towards this Government; and it is only after grave consideration, impelled by the strongest sense of duty, that I have asked of Congress the expression of its opinion on the subject.

I assure Senators that I have not presented these resolutions with any partisan purpose. I have not the shadow of a disposition to assault those to whom first and most immediately belongs the initiative in this business. It is perhaps true that special circumstances, and the more immediate concern of our people on the Pacific coast in the movements of France, furnish reasons why I should have watched French policy more carefully, and why I should feel more alarmed at its development, than most of those belonging either to the executive or legislative departments of the Government.

I do not hope to present all the facts and considerations that move me to my conclusions; if time permitted, the subject embraces too wide a field for any mere oral discussion. The most I have promised to myself has been to call the attention of Congress and the Government to the subject, and secure that consideration and action which I believe have been much too long delayed.

I have affirmed in these resolutions that the movement of France against Mexico is in violation of the known and recognized rules of international law, in violation of the treaty made at London between England, Spain, and France, in violation of repeated assurances given by France to this Government; and I now further affirm and will endeavor to satisfy the Senate that both the treaty and the assurances of which I speak were made on the part of France with the definite purpose of misleading and deceiving this Government; that they were designed as a fraud upon us, and that we have been misled, deceived, and defrauded to the very point of jeopardy by the Machiavelli who is now Emperor of the French.

What I have affirmed I shall now proceed to maintain as briefly as I find possible. I have said that this movement of France upon Mexico is in violation of the rules of international law. The true right and the extent of the right of France is briefly and well stated in a letter written by our minister at London to Mr. Seward, dated November 1, 1861, in which he says:

"There can be no doubt that, as it regards Europe, the voice of all the independent American nations is the same. They want no dictation, nor any resumption of their old relations. If they fail in performing their honest engagements, they make themselves liable in their property, but not in their persons or their political rights. Any attempt to transcend that broad line of distinction is a mere appeal to force, which can carry with it no obligation one moment beyond the period when it may be successfully overthrown. And the principle is broad enough to make the maintenance of it in one country equally the cause of all the rest."

It is unnecessary to elaborate the views expressed by our minister. The attempt in this civilized age, in this age of law, to make war upon and to overthrow a weak Government under the pretense of enforcing the payment of a money debt, is one that would not be dared by any other person than the dark, ambitious, and unscrupulous head of the French Government.

The terms of the treaty made at London are, I presume, familiar to Senators. Permit me, however, to call their attention to the second article; it reads:

"Art. 2. The high contracting parties bind themselves not to seek for themselves, in the employment of the coercive measures foreseen by the present convention, any acquisition of territory, or any peculiar advantage, and not to exercise in the subsequent affairs of Mexico any influence of a character to impair the right of the Mexican nation to choose and freely to constitute the form of its own Government."

It was understood that if Mexico did not to the extent of her reasonable ability adjust and provide for the respective claims of the three Powers, they would seize upon so much of the impost revenues of Mexico as would satisfy their demands. Further than this neither England nor Spain undertook to go; when France developed a policy foreign to this purpose they protested and withdrew. France, having used England and Spain to disguise her purposes, cover her landing, and establish her footing in Mexico; having committed England and Spain to what in them was folly but in France was ambition, the French movement is immediately changed into one of conquest and dominion.

That this attempt at conquest is a violation of the treaty of London and the assurances given to this Government, is a truth admitting of no discussion; but more than this; for it there is no shadow of justification or excuse. The fact is patent that this course France had determined on from the first; France had been dealing falsely with the allies and had dealt falsely with us; when the time was ripe she uncloaked herself, showing the brigand from top to toe.

And now, Mr. President, before entering upon particulars, and that the course of my remarks may be better understood, and as it is sufficiently understood that it was not a pecuniary enterprise that led France into Mexico, I will state what I undertand has induced this flagrant outrage upon public law, pledged faith, and the rights of a neighboring republic, and what I understand to be the programme of France, so far as it can be understood from what we know. The present constitutional government of Mexico is to be overthrown. Almonte, or some other instrument of French authority, is to be made temporary chief of the republic. France is to claim of the Government thus represented $27,000,000, together with the expenses incurred in the prosecution of the present war, say $100,000,000 more. Mexico has no means with which to pay this or any such amount. France will take territorial indemnity; that is, the Isthmus of Tehauntepec and the adjacent territory, the States bordering on the Rio Grande, Lower California, Sonora, and Sinaloa. This accomplished, the temporary chief, with the aid of what is known as the Church party in Mexico, supported by the bayonets of the French Emperor, will pronounce an Austrian prince Emperor of the Mexican people under the protectorate of Austria and France. This done, and while this is being done, France will confederate with the rebellion in the South. Even now I do not doubt such movement is in progress, if not consummated. She will then directly seek the possession and control of the territories south and west of the Mississippi river. It will not be long before the front of an undisguised enemy will be exhibited to this Republic; and simultaneous with that will be the attempt to seize upon all there is of our Republic on the shores of the Pacific. With the possession of the northern Pacific States of Mexico, and California and Oregon, together with the other possessions of France in the Pacific and the Indian ocean, she aims at the command of the ancient East, that vast country the exhaustless wealth of which has built up successively the richest and most powerful States of Europe, and to but a portion of which Great Britain is chiefly indebted for her ascendency both on sea and land, India has been the prize of many States. China is now the great prize of the nations. The three great Powers, Russia, France, and England, like three giant birds of prey, have been long hovering over that fated nation, watching each other and watching it. France would be strong upon the Pacific, that, if she cannot seize all, she may at least divide the prey.

In the time of the Cæsars in the city of Rome was accumulated a great part of the wealth of the known world. The unparalleled luxury of the Roman patricians of the first few centuries of our era took from Rome and the luxurious cities of the Mediterranean their gold and silver, much of which by caravans passed to India, and through India to China, then known as the land of silks; and while it is said that Nero had his house of gold, yet as early as the fifth century Rome was destitute of the precious metals. The precious metals, the moment they passed into the territories of China, remained and continued a part of the fixed possessions of the country. At the extreme of the world, holding all the rest of mankind barbarous, she only communicated with them to dispose of such things as in exchange for gold and silver would add to her wealth. The precious metals they never parted with; so that for at least eighteen centuries this process of accumulation has been continued. There is probably more gold and silver in the forms of moneyed wealth now in China than in all the States of Europe and America combined.

It is not strange that France should regard China with an avaricious eye. The French Emperor needs some such spoil as this to sustain his young authority and support his vast ambition. To accomplish this result, he needs a commanding position on the Pacific. He appears to be in the way of obtaining it, with our consent and at our sacrifice.

I have advanced these opinions as the general policy of France rather out of the regular line of argument; but thinking, perhaps, that from this statement the facts I shall present may be more readily applied.

I will now recur more directly to the questions presented by the resolutions. I have charged that the French Government gave us false and fraudulent assurances as to the intention of that Government toward Mexico.

It seems there was some anxiety felt by this Government on the subject of the movement of the allies. Our ministers at Paris, London, and Madrid were instructed to inquire as to the intention of the several Powers. In pursuance of instructions, Mr. Dayton called upon M. Thouvenel, French Minister of Foreign Affairs, and under date of September 27, 1861, Mr. Dayton writes Mr. Seward:

"He [M. Thouvenel] assured me, however, that whatever England and France might do, it would be done in reference to realizing their money debt only, and that they had no purpose whatever to obtain any foothold in Mexico, or to occupy permanently any portion of its territory. He repeated this with emphasis. He furthermore stated, explicity, that should Spain come in, as one of the Powers acting in concert with France and England, for her claims, it would be with a distinct understanding that she, too, should not attempt to hold any part of the territory. I was somewhat particular in my inquiries upon this point, because I could not forbear the belief that Spain might look to a reassertion of her former rule over Mexico or some part of it."

Here is a distinct assurance to the Government of the United States through its accredited minister, that France would do nothing more than assert her claim for her money debt. Again, on the 31st of March, 1862, in a letter from Mr. Dayton to Mr. Seward, he gives an account of another conversation on the subject with M. Thouvenel:

"I then referred M. Thouvenèl to your dispatch (No. 121) in reference to the action of the allies towards Mexico. He said France could do no more than she had already done, and that was to reassure us of her purpose not to interfere in any way with the internal government of Mexico. That their sole object was to obtain payment of their claims and reparation for the wrongs and injuries done to them."

Other assurances of a similar nature were continued to be given from time to time, evidently satisfying our amiable minister at the French Court, that Louis Napoleon was the most innocent and harmless man alive.

And now that our right to proper and truthful assurances may be well understood, I will call the attention of the Senate to an official correspondence between this Government and that of France, in 1826, during the Presidency of Mr. Adams, and while Mr. Clay presided over the State Department, Mr. Brown our minister at Paris, and M. Damas French Minister of Foreign Affairs. Our minister, in writing to Mr. Clay, states a conversation with the French minister, as follows:

"I then, in the most delicate and friendly manner, alluded to the French squadron which had appeared in the West Indies and on the American coast last summer, and stated that my Government would expect that, in case France should again send out a naval force disproportionate in the extent of its armament to the ordinary purpose of a peace establishment, its design and object should be communicated to the Government of the United States. The Baron de Damas answered, that the vessels comprising that squadron had been stationed at different places, where the number on each station was not more than sufficient for the service of protecting French commerce and their West India islands; that it had become necessary definitely to settle the relations between France and St. Domingo; that this squadron was hastily collected for that object, and that the nature of the service required secrecy. He said that it was not only right in itself, but had been customary with the French Government to communicate to friendly Governments, in time of peace, the objects of considerable fleets sent on distant service; that the peculiar circumstances in the instance I had alluded to had occasioned a departure from the rule, but that, in future, the United States should be duly apprised of the objects of every such squadron sent into their vicinity."

This was the policy of Mr. Adams and Mr. Clay, akin to the doctrine proclaimed by Mr. Monroe in 1823. In a letter to Baron Damas, Mr. Brown says:

PARIS, *January* 2, 1826.

"Sir: In the month of July last I had the honor to state to your excellency, with the utmost frankness, the views of the President of the United States in relation to the Spanish islands of Cuba and Porto Rico. I informed you that the United States could not see with indifference those islands passing from Spain to any other European power; and that the United States desired no change in their political or commercial condition, nor in the possession which Spain had in them. In the conference with which your excellency honored me on this day, I repeated the same assurances, and added, in a spirit of friendship, and with a view of guarding beforehand against any possible difficulties on the subject which might arise, that my Government could not consent to the occupation of those islands by any other Europern power than Spain, under any contingency whatever."

Was this a declaration of war? The French Minister of Foreign Affairs was told distinctly that this Government would not consent to the exchange of the authority of Spain for that of France or any other Government over Cuba and Porto Rico.

It was, then, the right of this Government to be informed, and to be truthfully informed, as to the purposes of France in Mexico; and nothing but purposes hostile to this Government can be inferred from deceitful and false representations. This right in us France admits; it follows France has purposely wronged us; France is hostile.

And now, Mr. President, as to the particular proof of the original bad faith of the French Government. I am inclined to think my assertion sufficiently sustained by the recently published letter of the French Emperor to General Forey, to be found in the morning papers, and which I shall read now, as having peculiar point in it so far as we are concerned. I will read his language:

"There will not be wanting people who will ask you why we go to lavish men and money for the establishment of a regular Government in Mexico. In the present state of the civilization of the world the prosperity of America is not a matter of indifference to Europe; for it is she who feeds our manufactories and gives life to our commerce. We have an interest in this, that the Republic of the United States be powerful and prosperous; but we have none in this, that she should seize possession of all the Mexican Gulf, dominate from thence the Antilles, as well as South America, and be the sole dispenser of the products of the New World."

France makes war to restrain our progress; she makes war upon a sister republic bordering upon our weakest and most valuable possessions; and I am told no voice must be raised here, either of warning to France, of sympathy for Mexico, or for counsel among ourselves. For myself, I will, for one, raise my voice not merely to warn, but to denounce, and I here denounce the proceedings of France as the most flagrant robber outrage that has been attempted by any modern civilized State; an outrage that challenges the condemnation of every other civilized State, and demands our interference; and if what I have to say fails at the present moment to reach the ears of those to whom I most immediately address myself, I will still trust it may be heard when there is some power and will in this Government to maintain the right.

It will require no skill in argument to justify any form of denunciation against France. She has made the truth of her own falsehood and wrong so patent that it cannot be disguised.

The relations of Almonte, the Mexican refugee, to this Government must be well known. As the confederate of Slidell and Mason, and as one of the conspirators in Europe against the integrity of the Union, he has played a conspicuous part. He is well known to have been a bitter enemy of this Government ever since he was made prisoner at the battle of San Jacinto. Driven from Mexico in 1857, he visits Europe to engage foreign arms in the overthrow of the constitutional Government of his country. To the Government of Spain he proposes the re-establishment of Spanish authority in Mexico. To Louis Napoleon he proposes the establishment of a monarchy under French protection. A shrewd and adroit politician, he secures a favorable hearing at both the courts of France and Spain. Spain dreams of her old dominion. France projects an Austrian alliance. The third Napoleon has a notion similar to that of the first Napoleon—an Austrian alliance, to be confederated with the oldest dynasty in Europe; to unite herself with the Power to which belongs the iron crown of Charlemagne; to join in firm alliance with the first Catholic Power in Europe. Such motives and such ambition drove Josephine into widowhood, and perhaps Napolean I into exile, and it is not beyond the range of possibility that the present emperor may find that in this his ambition has overleaped itself.

That the French Emperor undertook from the first to overturn the present Government and establish Maximilian upon a throne in Mexico is now openly avowed. In furtherance of this and other views, Almonte was taken under

French protection; but for his illness at the time he would have sailed with the French fleet. On his arrival in Mexico, he was escorted by French troops into the interior, against the remonstrances of the representatives of both the Spanish and English Governments. Under the protection of French bayonets, he had himself proclaimed chief of the republic. He was made, by the French authorities, the instrument to excite domestic revolution in aid of the arms of France. These facts appear in the diplomatic correspondence of this Government in relation to Mexican affairs furnished by the Secretary of State to this Congress. The same protection was afforded to the Padre Miranda, and was attempted in favor of Miramon, and would have been effeeted but for the violent interference of the English admiral. These facts are sufficient to prove that France designed overturning the existing Government, and purposed to deceive this Government by assurances to the contrary. But the climax of French outrage is to be found in the false and fraudulent pretexts set up by France as the justificaiion of her proceedings.

The entire monyed claim which France had any right to set up against Mexico amounted to but $190,000. A Swiss banker by the name of Jecker, by a fraudulent arrangement with the French minister resident in Mexico and Miramon, then the insurgent chief in possession of the capital, advanced to Miramon $750,000, for which Miramon caused to be issued $15,000,000 of Mexican bonds. The full payment of the $15,000,000 was one of the peremptory demands of the French Government. France made a further claim of $12,000,000 on general account, without item or specification, for wrongs done French citizens. The representatives of England and Spain protested against these claims as without the shadow of justice. England and Spain asked only a fair adjustment of actual claims, and a reasonable provision for payment. France not only demanded the $27,000,000, but whatever she might choose to claim as indemnity on account of her military operations. France demanded, and knew she was demanding, not only what was unjust, but what Mexico could not by any possibility perform. The English representatives consulted with the home Government, and the English Government remonstrated with the French. But the French Government persisted. Great Britain and Spain withdrew from the alliance, settled amicably their claims on Mexico, and withdrew from the Mexican territories, leaving France alone to pursue her long-determined scheme of conquest.

The outrageous nature of the French claim exhibited against Mexico can best be understood from an examination of the French ultimatum presented to the allies, and which first opened their eyes to the duplicity of the French Government. This ultimatum will be found in the English Blue Book, sent by the Queen to Parliament, in which the correspondence relating to this subject is much more full than in the correspondence furnished to Congress.

I call the attention of the Senate to this paper. It exhibits an outrage too great to be characterized. It not only offends the common sense of justice of mankind, but deserves execration every where and by all men. There is a further strange fact about this ultimatum. It appears to have been presented to the English and Spanish representatives, and when repudiated by them, without any demand in fact upon Mexico, or any effort at adjustment, France prepares for war. I will read the entire paper, for I wish this Government and people to understand the character of this Emperor of the French and his Government; what Mexico may expect, and what we too may expect, if his power proves equal to his will for mischief.

"The undersigned, representatives of France, have the honor, as stated in the collective note addressed this day to the Mexican Government by the plenipotentiaries of France, England, and Spain, to draw up as follows the ultimatum of which they have received orders in the name of the Government of his Majesty, the Emperor, to demand the pure and simple acceptance by Mexico—

"Art. 1. Mexico engages to pay France a sum of $12,000,000, at which amount are calculated the total French demands consequent upon events which have occurred up to July last, with the exceptions stipulated in articles two and four below. As regards those events which have taken place since the 31st July last, and of which a special reservation is here made, the amount of the claims against Mexico, to which they may give rise, will be fixed hereafter by the plenipotentiaries of France.

"Art. 2. The sums still due under the convention of 1853, which are not included in article one above, shall be paid to the rightful claimants in the form and allowing the terms of payment stipulated in the said convention of 1853.

"Art. 3. Mexico shall be held to the full, loyal, and immediate execution of the contract concluded in the month of February, 1859, between the Mexican Government and the firm of Jecker."

That is, they shall be held to a full and immediate payment of $15,000,000, for which Miramon only had received $750,000, by a fraudulent contract between himself, the French minister, and Jecker.

"Art. 4. Mexico is pledged to the immediate payment of the $11,000 forming the balance of the indemnity which was stipulated for in favor of the widow and children of M. Ricke, Vice Consul of France at Tepic, assassinated in October, 1859.

"The Mexican Government shall further, and according to the obligation already contracted by them, deprive of his rank and appointments, and punish in an exemplary manner, Colonel Rojas, one of the assassins of M. Ricke, with the express condition that Rojas shall not again be invested with any employment, command, or public functions whatsoever.

"Art. 5. The Mexican Government also engages to search out and to punish the authors of the numerous murders committed upon Frenchmen, and especially the murderers of M. Davesne."

Observe, it is stated generally, "numerous murders,"

"Art. 6. The authors of the attacks committed on the 14th of August last against the minister of the Emperor, and of the outrages to which the representative of France has been exposed in the first part of the month of November, 1861, shall be subjected to exemplary punishment; and the Mexican Government shall be bound to afford to France and to her representative the reparation and satisfaction due by reason of these deplorable excesses."

No such attack had, in fact, been made. They deal in general terms, and the reason why they deal in general terms is more patent from an examination of all the various provisions of this ultimatum:

"ART. 7. In order to insure the execution of the above articles five and six, and the punishment for all the outrages which have been or which may be committed against the persons of the Frenchmen residing in the republic, the minister of France shall always have the right of being present, whatever the case at issue, and by such representative as he may designate for that purpose, at all proceedings instituted by the criminal courts of the country.

"The minister shall possess the same right with regard to all criminal prosecutions instituted against his countrymen."

No criminal court can sit in Mexico for all time to come without a representative of the French Government on the bench. This is worse than the Austrians in Venetia.

"ART. 8. The indemnities stipulated in the present ultimatum shall bear a legal annual rate of interest of six per cent., to date from the 17th of July last and until their complete payment.

"ART. 9. As a guarantee for the accomplishment of the financial and other conditions laid down in the present ultimatum, France shall have the right of occupying the ports of Vera Cruz, of Tampico, and such other ports of the republic as she shall think fit; and of there establishing commissioners designated by the imperial Government, whose duty it shall be to take care that those Powers which have a legal claim shall receive such funds as are to be levied for their benefit on the produce of the maritime custom houses of Mexico, in fulfillment of the foreign conventions, and that French agents shall receive those sums which are due to France."

That is, France may occupy every port of Mexico.

"The commissioners in question shall, besides, be invested with the power of reducing, either by one-half or in a smaller proportion, according as they may judge advisable, the duties at present levied in the ports of the republic."

That is, they may reduce the duties to a nominal sum, postpone the payment of this debt forever, hold Mexico in a sort of peonage, commanding all her seaports, and, in fact, having her in absolute possession.

"It is expressly understood that merchandise which has already paid import duty shall in no case and on no pretext whatsoever, be subjected by the supreme Government or by the State authorities, to any additional custom duty, inland or otherwise, exceeding the proportion of fifteen per cent. on the duties paid on importation."

That is, France, having seized on all revenue derived from duties on imports, prevents Mexico from imposing any internal revenue on whatever foreign goods may be introduced, and can at her will break down all Mexican manufacturers.

"ART. 10. All measures which shall be judged necessary for regulating the apportionment among the parties interested of the sums levied upon the produce of the customs, as well as the manner and the periods of the payment of the indemnities above stipulated, as also for guarantying the execution of the conditions of the present ultimatum shall be framed in concert with the plenipotentiaries of France, England, and Spain."

This shows the character of that French faith in which it seems our minister at Paris and our Government here have so implicity trusted. With such a demand insisted upon by the French Government, and which is used only to drive off the allies, and is not even presented to Mexico; with such perfidy not only exhibited toward Mexico, but also toward ourselves, what may we not anticipate from France? We can anticipate nothing less than war. I insist that she is waging substantive war upon us now. It requires less than a prophet to predict open war the moment France has completed the required preparations for the onslaught.

Mr. President, I think I may be permitted to say that it is somewhat strange we should be found furnishing facilities to France to aid her in subjugating Mexico, while, at the same time, we have denied to Mexico like facilities. I do not understand it. It is said Mexico wants arms: France transportation. We cannot afford to part with arms. Let me ask, does not this Government require transportation as much as arms? If I am correctly informed, we have quite as great a demand for mules as for muskets to carry on our operations against the rebels.

Before proceeding further, however, in connection with the French ultimatum, I will refer to the Blue Book for a letter from Earl Cowley, at Paris, to Lord Russell, as to how the claims on Mexico were to be adjusted. It is of a piece with the ultimatum. Repeating his conversation with M. Thouvenel, Earl Cowley says:

"His excellency [M. Thouvenel] took this occasion to say that he could not consent to the appointment of a mixed commission, as had been suggested at one of the conferences at Vera Cruz, to arbitrate upon the demands of the three Governments; but he could not be averse to a proposal emanating from M. de Saligny, that a French commission, consisting of the French secretary of legation, the French consul at Vera Cruz, and a French merchant, should decide upon the merits of French claimants. If, after inquiry, it should be found that the aggregate amount of claims admitted by that commission was less than $12,000,000, of course that sum would be diminished in proportion."

The $12,000,000 of claims were not to be referred to any mixed commission, as an English and a French commission for example, but to three persons named: the secretary of Minister Saligny, who had been mixed up in these claims, the French consul at Vera Cruz, under his control, and a French merchant also under his control. This was the way in which justice was to be administered to Mexico at the point of French bayonets.

"I asked M. Thouvenel why M. de Saligny should not pursue the course adopted by Sir Charles Wyke is his project of ultimatum, and be satisfied with an engagement on the part of the Mexican Government, that all just claims not yet sent in should be paid. It must be admitted that M. Thouvenel's answer admits with difficulty of reply. What reliance, he asked, could be placed in any engagements of the kind after the experience which the allies had of Mexican faith? But I observed you must in some way or other trust a Mexican Government, for you do not suppose that the country is rich enough to pay off at once all the demands already made upon it, to say nothing of those which you have in store. Do you mean to remain there until every farthing shall have been paid? Our conversation terminated by M. Thouvenel observing, that while the Governments were discussing at home, events were marching in Mexico, and that it was very difficult to send instructions relating to matters which had occurred two months before the comments on them could be read."

This discussion is too plain to afford room for comment.

The chargé d'affaires of Mexico in Washington, in complaining to our Government of the attitude and course of this Government toward France and Mexico, is informed by our Secretary that he was not advised that war existed between France and Mexico. I desire to call the attention of the Senate to a letter written more than a year since by our minister at London to Mr. Seward. Mr. Adams writes:

"You will doubtless have had your attention drawn before this time to the course which the Mexican intervention is taking. On the reception of the news of the landing of the Spanish force and its occupation of Vera Cruz, the announcement is made of the outfit of a French force designed to follow up the advantage. It is no longer concealed that the intention is to advance to the capital, and to establish a firm government, *with the consent of the people*, at that place. But who are meant by that term does not appear. This issue is by no means palatable to the Government here, though it is difficult to imagine that they could have been blind to it. Feeble murmurs of discontent are heard, but they will scarcely be likely to count for much in the face of the obligation under which the action of the Emperor in the Trent case has placed them. The military occupation will go on, and will not cease with the limits now assigned to it. It is not difficult to understand the nature of the fulcrum thus obtained for operations in a new and a different quarter, should the occasion be made to use it. The expedition to the city of Mexico may not stop until it shows itself in the heart of the Louisiana purchase."

This letter was certainly a word of warning to our Secretary. The English Blue Book, to which the Secretary must have had access, shows that the French authorities regarded it as war from the time of the landing at Vera Cruz. This they have long since avowed. The letter of the minister is full of warning as to what is French policy. It would be well if Senators would carefully consider the substance of this letter. What with him was opinion has already proved to be fact, to the extent of the attempt by French officials, the representatives of the French Government, to obtain Texas by negotiation, with the Texan authorities in rebellion. The letter of our minister has the sound of different metal from the reply of our Secretary, who says;

"I shall carefully observe the progress of affairs in Mexico. If, indeed, our own Union were likely to fall, and the southern portion of the United States were to pass under a European protectorate, we could have small ground to hope that we could save Mexico from European reconquest and subjugation."

Again, taking counsel of his fears:

"But with reassurances of our own safety, comes up to us an absolute confidence that no part of the continent will lose republican institutions and self-government."

This is a strange letter in the presence of the warning of Mr. Adams and the facts already developed in Mexico. That France designed the establishment of a monarchy in Mexico was understood in diplomatic circles throughout Europe, and was common tea-table gossip throughout the United States. It had been particularly stated in the English Parliament, and was not in terms denied anywhere. I have before me a work, entitled "Mexico in 1861–62," by Mr. Lempriere, an English gentleman, in which is quoted a part of a debate in Parliament on this subject. This subject is one that may be debated in the British Parliament, but not in the American Senate. In the House of Commons, Mr. Fitzgerald remarked:

"Had her Majesty's Government no warning of those views being held by the French Government? M. Thouvenel, in one of his despatches, said: 'We do not wish to interfere; but we think that the presence of our forces there will give that moral support to the monarchical feeling which we believe to exist, and that there will be a chance and opportunity for the establishment of a new and regenerated Government.'"

Mr. Fitzgerald in complaining that before the treaty of London England was advised of the policy of France to establish a monarchy, at least to reorganize the Government in Mexico. He goes on to say:

"It was idle to say, when Almonte was constantly coming to this country, and communicating with the Government and with public bodies, and after the language of M. Thouvenel—it was idle to say that the Government had not a distinct warning that it was the intention of the French Governmet to interfere in the internal affairs of Mexico, and possibly to establish a new form of Government."

I will now leave the question as to what this Government should have known, and return to the subject of French faith, as I wish there to be no misunderstanding as to the facts upon which I rest my conclusions. I have before me a letter from Admiral Dunlop written to Vice Admiral Sir A. Milne, under date of March 4, 1862, a portion of which I will read.

"SIR: With reference to a letter to you from the Secretary of the Admiralty, relative to a large party in Mexico being in favor of a monarchial form of government, and that there is an intention of calling the Archduke Ferdinand Maximilian to the throne, I have the honor to inform you that the subject having been mentioned to me by Vice Admiral Jurieu de la Graviére, when I first met him at Havana, I have taken every means in my power to ascertain whether their are any good grounds for supposing that any influential party in Mexico is in favor of a monarchy, and the information I have obtained from the best sources within my reach leads me to suppose that the only party in Mexico at all in favor of a monarchy is the Church party, and that merely because it sees no other prospect whatever of regaining influence with the Mexican people.

"2. The Church party embraces all that is bigoted and fanatical in the country, and is therefore retrogressive in policy and at variance with the spirit of the age; and it is detested by a great majority of the people, who are in favor of a liberal policy."

I read this that it may be understood what were the views of an English monarchist in regard to the true sentiments of the Mexican people, and to show whether or not it is true that the Emperor Napoleon III is in fact lending aid to the majority of that people for the purpose of establishing a firm Government. Now, let me read from a letter of Earl Russell to Sir Charles Wyke, on the same question, as to the policy of the French Government:

"The difference which has arisen between the French Government on the one side, and the British and Spanish Governments on the other, is greatly to be deplored; yet it is to be remarked that it is a difference rather as to facts than as to principle. The French embassador, by order of his Government, signed most willingly the convention of the 31st of October, by which the allies pledged themselves not to interfere with the right of the people of Mexico to choose their own form of government. But the emperor and his Government appear to be persuaded that the name of Ferdinand Maximilian put forth by General Almonte, will produce a general burst of enthusiasm in Mexico, and a universal adhesion to that prince in the provinces. Now, either this is an error, or it is not."

* * * * * * * * * *

"The only apprehension of a serious kind which I entertain is, that the French general, anxious for the cause of monarchy and of Catholic unity, may lend the aid of the French arms to the reactionary party in Mexico, and thus give fresh life to the civil war, which appears at present to have almost died away."

When the civil war had, in fact, died away; when the regular constitutional Government was in full authority; when all the leading men of the reactionary party had been driven forth into exile, then comes the French Government, apparently with the support of England and Spain, to overturn the Government that had then the appearance of stability, and certainly had constitutional form and authority. France comes forward to overthrow that Government, and establish a monarchy in its stead. This purpose again appears more particularly from the *procès verbal* had at Orizaba, after the difference between the allies, for the purpose of preserving the causes of their several complaints and difference. I quote from the Blue Book. "The Count de Reus"—the same with General Prim, the Spanish commander—

> "The Count de Reus then questions M. de Saligny respecting a personal transaction; the latter appears to have said to Colonel Menduina, Governor of Vera Cruz, and to M. Cortes, consul for Spain in the port, that the Count de Reus only found fault with the projects of Mexican monarchy in favor of the Archduke because he himself aspired to get himself crowned Emperor of Mexico; and he appears even to have declared that he possessed proof of this. The Count de Reus exclaims loudly against such an assertion, and summons his colleague to give explanations on the subject, adding that such an absurb report in the mouth of the public would not have possessed any importance, but that coming from M. de Saligny it required a serious aspect; and that, lastly, if the proofs existed of this he insisted on their production.
>
> "The French commissioner remembers, it is true, having spoken in this sense; but he only repeated what was publicly reported."

The minister, Saligny, here admits he had stated that the only reason why the Count de Reus found fault with Maximilian, was that he, De Reus, wished to be king himself, admitting his own position and that of his Government by the very statement. It was well understood that this was French policy at an early day, and the proof of it runs through both the American and English correspondence on Mexican affairs. It is strange our Secretary could not see it. It is, then, unquestionably true that France, first averring to the world and assuring us that she had no purpose to more than collect a mere money debt due French citizens, at the same time designed, under cover of false, fraudulent, and unfounded pretexts, the subjugation of Mexico, and the placing upon a throne to be established in Mexico an Austrian prince.

I think I have done with so much of the discussion. I will now discuss what I regard as other points of French policy.

France has no country affording a home supply of the precious metals. It is otherwise with Russia, Austria, and England, as also with this Republic. France has no considerable colonial possessions to which she can direct her own emigrating population and at the same time add to the strength of France. She has no such countries tributary as are India, Australia, and Canada to England. From the time of Richelieu she has sought to build up a colonial and commercial policy, from and by which to derive wealth and strength to the central State, and during the same time to secure a country producing largely the precious metals, with a view to control both their use and direction. In the pursuit of her policies, France has always been the most unscrupulous and aggressive of the modern European States.

What cause had France for her assault upon the Sandwich Islands, except to get the possession of a certain commanding commercial position in the Pacific ocean? What for her assault upon the natives of the Society Islands? What for her taking possession of the island of New Caledonia, when it was not her right by discovery or by any of the laws of nations? What for her aggressive war against the Annamites, the people of Cochin China? What for her outrageous assault upon the King of Siam but two or three years since? What, but a determination to get certain commanding positions without regard to right, without regard to law, but for the benefit and strength of the central Government of France? What right had France in Africa; and for what purpose, but to gratify the mob of Paris, was that brave Prince of the desert, Abdel Kader, brought from his native plains a captive, as was once a British king to grace a Roman triumph? Perhaps he contemplates making Juarez, the distinguished patriot and chief of the Mexican republic, a similar exhibition, with which to feast the eyes of French curiosity. All these several acts of invasion have been made regardless of right, without it be the robber's right; and the crime of robbery is not diminished because done in the name of kings or emperors.

I will now approach matters nearer home. The possession of the territories, now part of the United States on the Pacific, was contemplated by the first Napoleon. The French voyageurs and trappers from Canada and Louisiana, traveled, trapped and hunted from the Russian possessions in the north to the Gulf of California. Among these persons, our own mountain men, and even the Indian tribes, are still to be found the evidences of his policy. In 1839 Marshal Soult, then Prime Minister to Louis Philippe, detached M. Duflot de Mofras from the Legation at Madrid, and assigned him to the legation in Mexico, with instructions to examine and report upon the value and condition of the Pacific coast from the Gulf of California north. His work was published in Paris in 1844, in two volumes. His business was to ascertain the facilities and advantages of planting French establishments upon that coast. The advantages to France for commercial purposes, particularly in relation to the prospective trade with China and Japan, in securing a position in California and Oregon, as well as the islands of the Pacific, are set forth in the strongest terms. In writing of California he says:

> "It is evident to us that California may belong to whatever nation may choose to send there a sloop-of-war and two hundred men."

And again:

> "Of all this vast extent of country, comprised between the equator and Behring's straits, the southern part of Oregon and Upper California form the portion which by its central position seems destined to acquire the greatest importance."

Here, what was temptation for the French King is now infinitely more tempting to the French Emperor.

In 1850 the French Government, under the pretext of disbanding and providing for a portion of the *Garde Mobile*, fitted out and sent to California a large body of these experienced soldiers, who were immediately taken under the protection and patronage of M. Dillon, then French consul at San Francisco. The heavy emigration of our own people from this side of the mountains was not then anticipated by France. The political nature of this movement has been well understood in California. A large body of experienced French veterans, supported by a large French emigration, an emigration favored by the Government of France, under the management of the French representative, a man of consummate address and talent, was sufficient to arrest the attention of even a looker-on in California. The people of San Francisco had some taste of the quality of these gentlemen of the sword in the unfortunate disturbances of 1856. These French soldiers, to a man, took up arms against the authorities and the laws, and a wilder and fiercer set of desperadoes never established any reign of terror. They insisted on taking the city prison by assault, they demanded a wholesale slaughter of obnoxious citizens, and particularly the city and State officials, and from the first, until finally disbanded, their watchword was revolution. Their demand for lives, and a revolutionary movement throughout the State, alarmed every good citizen connected with the movement, of which they made so prominent a feature, and but for this timely alarm they would have caused the streets of the city of San Francisco to run red with blood. But France has not rested with establishing a military and physical power in California; in addition to this military nucleus and a large French emigrant population, she has promoted the establishment of a French moneyed power in that State. Through the system of moneyed associations organized in Paris, the capital to be used in California, that State is almost as badly mortgaged to the French as Mexico was to the Church and the monasteries. I state these things not merely to indicate French policy on the Pacific, but to show further that France is now a latent power in our Pacific possessions.

But there is more to be said in this connection.

The expedition started, in 1852, by the French Count de Raousset-Boulbon was at the instance of the French consul, one of the ablest diplomats France has ever had abroad; and it met with the direct countenance and assistance from the French minister plenipotentiary in Mexico. De Raousset-Boulbon organized his well-armed party of Frenchmen in California, went down to Sonora, boasting to a friend of mine in San Francisco that, if successful in his undertaking, he would "send a ship to France which would buy the empire." He quarreled with the Mexican Governor of Sonora, attacked him in Hermosillo, the principal city of the State, and captured the place. He was, however, too weak in numbers to hold the State, and did not, as he probably expected, find the people ready to accept his rule; so he made terms with Governor Blanco, extorted a sum of money from him sufficient to defray the expenses of his party back to California, and temporarily abandoned Sonora, predicting a speedy return, with better results.

In those days Santa Anna was playing, or attempting to play, in Mexico the same game so successfully carried on by Louis Napoleon in France. Santa Anna commenced his progress by adopting the title of "*Serene Highness*," and doubtless had the high approval of Louis Napoleon's minister in Mexico. The wily and sagacious chieftain summoned the bold and talented De Raousset-Boulbon to his capital, and appointed him colonel in the Mexican army; and with this commission he returned to California, with the purpose of organizing a French force of three thousand men for the occupation of Sonora, Lower California, and Sinaloa, and thus to gain the control of the sea of Cortes. As was well stated by the *Revue des deux Mondes*, "perhaps he himself dreamed of the empire of Mexico."

The enlistment, organizing, and arming of this force proceeded in California under the patronage of Monsieur Dillon, the French consul, and that of Santa Anna's vice consul at the same port. The attention of our Government was attracted to the movement, and General Wool promptly took measures to ascertain its bearings and its extent. Dillon became alarmed and published a proclamation, carefully worded, which, while it would save the appearance of complicity on the part of the French Emperor, would not seriously injure the prospects of the enterprise. He cautioned all French subjects to carefully abstain from joining any expedition which would place them out of the reach of their Government's protection, but at the same time professed in private to see nothing illegal in De Raousset's enterprise. A large ship, the Challenge, one of the best ships that ever sailed from our harbor, had been chartered, and was nearly ready for sea, when the American Government seized her. The Mexican vice consul was arrested and tried before the United States district court for a violation of the neutrality laws.

The French consul, Dillon, was subpenaed to appear before the judge of the United States district court. He refused to appear and give his testimony. The judge issued his warrant or writ of attachment against his person to bring him before the court; and the chairman of the Committee on Foreign Relations will remember how fiercely Monsieur Sartiges fought out with Mr. Secretary Marcy the indignity claimed to have been heaped on the Government of France, because it had been sought to make Dillon a witness concerning an expedition of which he had been the master spirit. It is true, France repudiated that in her public journals, but those persons who then lived in the country, and who understood the records of the courts of justice of the day, knew that the reverse of those French statements was the truth; that it was an expedition gotten up to take Sonora by the French Government, using the same force that had been sent out originally from the *Garde Mobile* to revolutionize and take possession of California. Of the whole force, only about three hundred Frenchmen were on board the ship Challenge at the time of her seizure. This party only sailed. Our Government had acted deficiently in maintaining her neutrality laws to that extent in this instance.

And here I must with sadness allude to the action of our Government at that time, which allows of a suspicion that even then treason was lurking in the hearts of men high in place and power. Mr. Jefferson Davis was then Secretary of War. The vigorous action of General Wool against the breakers of the law of neutrality was disapproved by the Secretary, and he was so hampered by the contradictory action of the War Department that his power for wholesome action in the matter was nearly destroyed. The Challenge stole from the harbor of San Francisco while De Raousset-Boulbon was under surveillance by the military authorities. Further recruiting for the expedition was abandoned, and subsequently the leader, taking advantage of a storm, escaped on a small vessel, and after a long and severe voyage, joined his battalion in Guaymas, Sonora. At that time General Yanez was military commandant of the Mexican forces in Sonora. A patriotic man, he was opposed to the projects of Santa Anna, and, while he obeyed the order of the central power to receive the French troops under *Colonel* De Raousset-Boulbon, he carefully abstained, on the one hand from assigning them to any separate duty apart from the Mexican soldiers, and on the other hand, he caused them to be promptly paid every week to prevent any pretexts for mutiny. De Raousset found himself, therefore, confined to performing garrison duty in a sea-port town, instead of holding an indepedent command in the sparsely populated interior, where he could easily consummate his plans of conquest. The battalion remained inactive week after week, the colonel applying almost daily for orders. But the Mexican general maintained his policy, treating the French commander with all the respect due to his grade, and issuing orders to him and his troops in connection with the native officers and soldiers. Finally De Raoussett *demanded* that he should be furnished with artillery and sent to the frontier. The general quietly informed him that when he desired his services on the frontier he would give him his orders and prescribe his armaments. Hopeless of success by other means, so long as Yanez held command in Sonora, De Raoussett-Boulbon boldly mutinied, seized two pieces of artillery, and attempted to take possession of the place. His soldiers, almost to a man, fought desperately under his orders, but after a severe conflict the Mexican troops, with the assistance of the local militia, triumphed, and the count surrendered himself and party as prisoners, he nobly refusing to make terms for himself, but providing that his soldiers should be well treated and sent out of the country. He was condemned and shot at Guaymas, on the 12th of August, 1854, and his men were soon sent back to California by the Mexican Government.

Thus ended, disastrously, the second attempt of France for the conquest of northwestern Mexico, which she is now attempting with larger and more certain means, and in a more direct manner.

The consul Dillon, whose particular business it had been for many years to superintend French interests on the Pacific, was now withdrawn from San Francisco, and made consul general of the West Indies. The Isthmus of Tehuantepec, a canal through Nicaraugua, and a more direct movement upon Mexico, induced the French Emperor to change the base of his operations from the Pacific to the Gulf of Mexico. France had determined to control Mexico. The idea of a French-Austrian monarchy may have been an after-thought. The skillful and fraudulent diplomacy of France deceived England and Spain into a partial coöperation, and deceived this Government into a polite, if not submissive, acquiescence. It would seem that with all her cunning arts and disciplined arms, France has thus far failed. If it is true, as reported, that the French troops have been twice defeated, and the French fleet driven from the little port of Acapulco, perhaps it may prove wise for the ambitious Emperor to consider whether or not, while he is endeavoring to subjugate the free people of Mexico, his own people may not undertake to subjugate him. Still, it may be true that now, in the face of defeat, he will not dare abandon his enterprise; we, indeed, are informed that fifteen thousand of the Imperial Guard, the choicest troops of France, are ordered out as reinforcements. The city of the Montezumas is nevertheless still in the distance; and I trust that long before its streets and palaces, are commanded by French artillery, if Mexico needs aid, she may receive sufficient aid from this Republic.

This question of our duty to render efficient aid to Mexico is no mere question of the Monroe doctrine. If the rule laid down by Mr. Monroe in his messages of December 1823 and 1824 is a wise and just one, demanded by a just consideration both of our rights and interests, it follows, by a much stronger reason, that the duty is now devolved upon this Government to protest against and, if necessary, resist by force of arms the extension of the power and policies of France, with the monarchial institutions of Europe, over the neighboring republic of Mexico.

There has been much dispute of late years as to the extent of the Monroe doctrine, and exactly as to what condition of facts it applies. In 1856 it was claimed to apply to the affairs of Central America by some of our public men; by others it was denied; but the doctrine, as laid down and applied by Mr. Monroe, has become established law, not disputed on this continent, and it has from time to time been acquiesced in by the principal States of Europe.

The Spanish American States had achieved a successful revolution, and established in the place of Spanish rule republican institutions. The alliance of European Powers, known as the Holy Alliance, looked to the maintenance of legitimacy everywhere, and claimed the "undoubted right to take a hostile attitude in regard to those States, in which the overthrow of the Government may operate as an example." The recovery of the revolted colonies of Spain was embraced in the scope of their determination; and in 1823 the Conde de Ofalia, Spanish minister of foreign affairs, addressed a circular letter to the Courts of Paris, St. Petersburg and Vienna, in the name of his "august master," inviting a conference at Paris, to the end that the allies might aid his Catholic Majesty "in adjusting the affairs of the revolted countries of

America." To this conference Great Britain was invited, but declined in most unequivocal terms.

President Monroe, in his message in 1823, speaking of the Spanish American colonies, whose independence we had already recognized, remarks:

"We owe it to candor and to the amicable relations existing between the United States and those Powers (allies) to declare that we should consider any attempt on their part to extend their system to any portion of this hemisphere as dangerous to our peace and safety. With the existing colonies or dependencies of any European Power we have not interfered, and shall not interfere; but with the Governments who have declared their independence, and maintained it, and whose independence we have, on great consideration, and on just principles, acknowledged, we could not view any interposition for the purpose of oppressing them, or controlling in any other manner their destiny by any European Power, in any other light than as a manifestation of an unfriendly disposition towards the United States."

In the same message, the President further remarks:

"It is impossible that the allies should extend their political system to any portion of either continent (North or South America) *without endangearing our peace and happiness.*" * * "It is equally impossible, therefore, that we should behold such interposition in any form with indifference."

Again, in his message of 1824, President Monroe, speaking of the Spanish American States, remarks:

"But in regard to our neighbors our situation is different. It is impossible for the European Governments to interfere in their concerns, especially in those alluded to, which are vital, without affecting us; indeed, the motive which might induce such interference in the present state of the war between the parties, if a war it may be called, would appear to be equally applicable to us."

The last expression I quote is the same in substance with the warning given by our Minister at London, Mr. Adams, and which I have already quoted. It is the same principle and doctrine maintained by the succeeding Administration of President Adams, in the correspondence with the French Government to which I have also referred, and the full justice of which was then admitted by France.

As a complement to the quotations I have made from President Monroe, I will read a scrap of history from the North American Review, for April, 1856. The writer has been referring to the period when Spain had applied to the allies for their coöperation in recovering the revolted Spanish American colonies:

"At this juncture of events, and just before the annual opening of the English Parliament, the message of President Monroe arrived in Europe, and by its well-weighed and explicit language on Spanish-American affairs, coupled with the refusal of England to take part in the proposed congress, 'effectually put an end to the project of assembling one similar to those which had met at Vienna, Aixla-Chapelle, Laybach and Verona.' Such, at least, is the testimony of Mr. Stapleton, in his 'Political Life of the Right Honorable George Canning.' Mr. Brougham, in his address on the king's speech at the opening of the parliamentary session on February 3, 1824, spoke of the arrival in Europe of President Monroe's message as an event by which 'the question with regard to South America, he believed, was disposed of, or nearly so, and than which no event had ever dispersed greater joy, exultation and gratitude, over all the freemen of Europe.' At a later day in the same session, on the 18th of March, Lord John Russell contrasted its 'decided language' with the fluctuating policy of the British ministry as represented at Verona."

The policy indicated by Mr. Monroe has continued to be the fixed, uniform and unbending policy and law of conduct of this Government down to the time of the movement of the allies under the treaty at London and the present French movement. The political necessity of adhering to it has not been disputed in this country, while its wisdom has been admitted and commended as well in Europe as America.

Is it radical weakness in our Government; is it want of will in those who administer our Government; is it because we are weaker to maintain a policy than we were forty years ago; is it because we cannot, should not, or will not, that we seem to ignore the wisdom and experience of the past and yield a cardinal doctrine approved, and well approved, for near one half a century?

I see no radical weakness in the Government; we are stronger now for foreign war than we were forty years ago. We can lend all the aid required to maintain the integrity and independence of Mexico. In 1823, the Holy Alliance, the combined strength of the continental Powers of Europe, threatened interference. We firmly advised them, in substance, "then you are at war with us." All Europe paused, and then abandoned the projected enterprise. France now stands alone; and I undertake to say, that if all continental Europe was now combined in the common purpose of subjugating Mexico, and placing a European prince upon the Mexican throne, with all our domestic difficulties upon our shoulders, we still are strong enough to maintain ourselves and Mexico. Our difficulties do not change the rule of our duty, nor relieve us from resisting, to the extremity of most sanguinary war, the overthrow of a republic on our borders by the arms of a European potentate, and the establishment in its place of a European monarchy. Let those who, taking counsel of their fears, and having the power to act in this matter, yet tamely and silently yield, and particularly countenance such disastrous results, await the time, soon to come, when France shall strike direct at us; and I assure them they will find the wilderness and the desert places more comfortable for them than national council halls or places where our people most do congregate.

The States of Europe are not so strong against us as some seem to fear. The emperors and kings of Europe stand in slippery places. The present power of France or Austria is not possessed, even if at present commanded by either emperor. To truly possess the power they seek to continue to command, demands that the experiment of free government on this continent shall prove a failure, and to secure the result of such a failure is now nearer to the interests, and commands more of the consideration of those two emperors and their counselors, than either the affairs of Italy or the balance of Europe. Mexico is to-day less the object of the present French aggression than the dismemberment and overthrow of the powerful Republic of the United States of America. When anarchy shall have fully taken the place of the order that once prevailed throughout our States their thrones will cease to tremble. This Republic has been the example to all the lovers of freedom throughout the world. To it is attributed the several revolutions in France and all the struggles of Germany to realize free government. It is not strange that in this time of our tribulation they should seek to demonstrate the insufficiency of republican institutions for the maintenance of an organized and powerful State. At any day a question may be raised between emperor and people. I believe that question will be raised in France whenever for just cause this Republic is forced into a war with the administration of the emperor. But, independent of this, should it prove true that this Republic, the most prosperous the world has seen, the people of which enjoyed every blessing government could provide, has been destroyed, has failed to maintain unity with order, and has sunk into anarchy, then who will deny that a monarchy and a nobility are not necessities? The oppressed multitudes will cease to struggle up against oppression. There will be no place upon which even the philosopher will dare to plant his foot. He cannot even dream of free government now or in the years to come.

I have heard it stated that Louis Napoleon is friendly to this Government; that those who control French governmental action are favorable to this Republic. I have heard it stated that our Secretary of State, who directs our correspondence with France, relies upon the friendly assurances of the representative of the French Court at Washington. The chairman of the Committee on Foreign Relations, in objecting to this discussion, tells us France is constant in her expressions of friendship. Mr. President, if gentlemen are not smitten with judicial blindness; if they can observe anything of the public movements of the day, they cannot fail to see that equally with the leaders of rebellion in the South, the Emperor of France is our determined and dangerous enemy. What is true of the Emperor is true of his Court. Senor de la Fuente, the late minister of Mexico at Paris, upon his return truly reported that if one of our citizens being in Paris should claim that this Republic enjoyed the favor of France he would be laughed at for his ignorance. From the day Napoleon ascended to power as emperor, he has, in fact, exhibited a hostile aspect. As early as 1855 the desire of the emperor to break peace with this country was openly asserted to some of our officers in Paris by French officials high in place and power. Napoleon wants cotton fields, gold fields, fields for home emigration, a transit by the Isthmus to the Pacific; the commanding position on the Pacific; access to and the control of eastern commerce; above and beyond all this, he desires to see the free institutions of this Republic overthrown. Texas, Louisiana west of the Mississippi, and the Terre Caliente of Mexico, will answer for his cotton fields. California and Sonora will answer for his gold fields, as well as for his home emigration. Either Tehuantepec or Nicaraugua will answer for his transit to the Pacific. The Pacific coast from Mazatlan to the Columbia, with the great bay of San Francisco, secures him, as against any power in the world, the command of the Pacific and the direction and control of the trade of China and Japan. When Louis Napoleon shall have been permitted to do these things w shall have ceased to be a nation.

I shall now, Mr. President, approach more particularly the relation of California, Oregon, Arizona and to the French possession of Mexico. The States of Sonora and Lower California border on our possessions. They both possess salubrious climates; both abound in mineral wealth; and the extensive and fertile valleys of Sonora are capable of supporting a numerous population; they embrace both sides of the Gulf of California, which they command as well as the mouth of the Colorado. Guaymas is one of the best ports on the Pacific, convenient for trade between Europe and the East by the way of Cape Horn or the Isthmus. If Sonora and Lower California become French territories, the port of San Diego is nearer by land to the French possessions by four hundred miles than is San Francisco. The southern part of our State of California is none too loyal, and many of our disaffected citizens have moved down into Arizona and Sonora. Our coast is without even harbor defenses; we could not at San Francisco accomplish what is reported as performed at Acapulco. As for field artillery, small arms and ammunition, we have scarcely sufficient for the purposes of our Indian frontier. It may be substantially affirmed that we are bare of anything like means for even defensive war. A large French fleet is now visiting the ports of Mexico and California, and to-day commands our coast. It has been stated for months, and it has not been contradicted, that eight thousand French troops have sailed for Sonora. With eight thousand veteran troops and a well appointed fleet what may we not have to fear, particularly for the city of San Francisco, the harbor of San Diego, and the entire southern half of the State? The important port of San Diego, once rivalling San Francisco, is at any time at their mercy.

A glance at the map will show that France can land troops and their supplies on the Colorado within five days' easy march of San Diego, threatening its rear. How is such a movement to be resisted? Where are the fortifications or intrenchments or cannon to guard San Diego from such an attack? Where are the men and the arms which at a month's notice, even, not to say one week's notice, could be collected to oppose such a movement? They do not exist. San Diego once taken, France would have an excellent safe harbor through which her forces might be indefinitely reinforced and supplied by sea. And thence an army could move up our coast, capturing every port in California from the rear, and rendering useless expensive sea-coast fortifications.

California is strong in brave men, but weak in material of war—weak in the means of producing that material. We have certainly not arms enough in California to arm ten thousand men. I do not believe we have any more arms than are now in the hands of the troops who have been called into the Federal service. We have no rifled field artillery; we have no founderies for cannon; we have no powder mills; we have none of the preparations for war. With Arizona in hostile possession, with the forts of western Mexico in possession of hostile fleets sufficiently powerful to prevent communication by sea between Panama and California, how could the Government, using every endeavor, afford the relief of a single gun, musket, or a round of ammunition to our State?

Is there not danger, then, in this movement of Napoleon? Is it not well to look this danger full in the face and provide against it, rather than, through cowardice, or prudence, if you please, to abstain from discussion and preparation lest we should, perchance, offend the sensibilities of his Imperial Majesty of France?

Suppose, for the sake of argument, that the Emperor of France is peculiarly friendly to us and our institutions—rather a violent supposition, I think—yet is it wise to give any foreign Power such a tempting opportunity to act upon our weakness?

I feel that I know the purposes of France toward this country, and particularly her purpose to seize on California, and I regard it as my duty, as well as right, to demand for the subject proper regard and proper action. French policy and purposes are understood in California as I understand them. I will read an extract from the most representative paper on our coast, the Sacramento Union, and a true Union paper, as it purports to be. The paper is of the date of December 15, 1862:

"The increase of the French naval force in the Pacific is not explained by the necessities of a war between France and Mexico. A single war vessel at each port would answer the purpose of a blockade. *L'Echo du Pacifique*, the French journal at San Francisco, which has enjoyed support and protection under our flag for about eleven years, speaks of the approach of 'our fleet,' and expresses the hope that 'our admiral' will not be compelled to adopt severe measures to check an alleged illicit traffic between San Francisco and the Mexican ports. This is suggestive of the possibility of complications growing out of the interference of these French men-of-war with American trade. And it is not improbable that, if the situation were favorable, even the ready and convenient apology of our silky Secretary would not save us from serious encroachment."

The French consul at San Francisco is a very important officer and has charge of all the French policy. He is not a mere commercial agent, but the representative of the French Government, and the *Journal l'Echo du Pacifique* is his organ, and speaks from his office:

"The proposed occupation of Sonora by a French division may have no significance prejudicial to American interests; but if England were to send that number of troops to Canada, her recognized colony, an explanation would be demanded. When we consider the location of Sonora, and the turbulent element existing in southern California hostile to our national Government, in connection with the concentration of a powerful French fleet on this coast, we are forced to regard the situation as one that demands the earnest attention of the Government and the adoption of prompt precautionary measures."

We regard this movement with great apprehension. This paper expresses the sentiments and apprehensions, if you please, of the people of California on the subject. We talk of those things we understand; and here I wish to state what I have long observed, that we seem to understand everything that is east of us, scarce anything that is west. The gentlemen from the Atlantic seaboard seem to understand more about what is transpiring in France and England than about anything that is beyond the mountains. By some law, which I will not undertake to expound, our people hardly ever understand anything that is further west than they have been. It has been and is a matter of grave and just complaint that the condition of California, its necessities, could not be understood at Washington; and what has been formerly true is especially true so far as our present military conditioned is concerned, and particularly our danger from French aggression.

Because we have a change of Administration every four years and with it a change of policy, our public men seem to think there is no such thing as state policies. The old Governments of the world have their fixed and persistent policies, which even revolutions do not change. Much of the present policy of France you may study back to the time of Richelieu. To our neglect of something like fixed policies may be traced our internal disturbances and the fact that France now threatens us. If the Monroe doctrine had been firmly asserted in the fall of 1861, there would be no French troops now in Mexico and no danger of a French invasion of our own territories. If letters of marque had been promptly issued, our volunteer force for the ocean been promptly called out, there would have been no confederate pirates on the high seas and no running of our blockades.

If the principles enunciated by President Jackson in his proclamation to the people of South Carolina had been reasserted in 1860 and 1861, the peace of the Union would not have been disturbed. We have had sufficient policies instituted, but, either through ignorance, or folly, or weakness, or wickedness, they have not been pursued. Let me ask, what is the cause this has been so? Is this same want of purpose or policy to continue?

Now, Mr. President, I have shown first that France has violated the law of nations, as well laid down by our present minister at the British Court. I have shown by paper and by record her violation of the terms of the treaty made at London, and her repeated assurances given to this Government. I have shown that she has been acting in fraud of this Government, and commenced with falsely stating her purposes. I have shown that she has undertaken, without cause and against every rule of justice, by a course of proceeding which offends the common sense of justice of mankind, to subjugate the people of Mexico for her own profit, and not only for that purpose, but to prevent any increase of power on our part on this continent. I say France has nothing to do with our increase of power on this continent, no more than we have to do with her treaty as to whether she shall have Nice, or whether it shall belong to the States of Italy. I have shown that she has committed herself to the establishment in Mexico of a monarchy of the Austrian line. I have, I think, satisfactorily shown that, while establishing a monarchy in Mexico irrespective of the will of the people, she has a policy which involves her own immediate occupation of a part of the present territories of Mexico, and that she is now undertaking a policy whereby she expects to seize a part of the domain which at the present time belongs to this Confederacy. The fact which is not disputed, that her diplomatic agents have been feeling the way to see whether they cannot get possession of Texas, independent of the southern confederacy, proves this. The fact that she has been struggling for years to occupy California proves this. Her movements upon Sonora prove this. Her treachery in getting fraudulent entry into Mexico proves all this, and more.

With these facts before us, shall we tamely abandon a policy more important than any one of our fundamental laws; a policy we had regarded as established, and as essential to our own as well as all free institutions; a policy, the bare affirmation of which served as a perfect shield over the Spanish American States, sufficient to protect them from the arms of banded continental Europe; a policy which a great English statesman declared had "dispensed the greatest joy, exultation, and gratitude over all the freemen of Europe?" Shall we, I say again, merely take counsel of our fears, and yield not only an established policy, but a great principle, the maintenance of which is demanded of us by the very laws of self-preservation?

For what shall we do this? If any one says that either policy or necessity demands or requires such a course, I here deny the statement. We have not as yet even remonstrated with France; but suppose we require of her the withdrawal of her troops from Mexico, and the demand is denied; give arms, authority, and the flag of the Union to the people of California, and California will send twenty thousand loyal, brave and tried men, men worthy to bear our flag; and when the folds of that flag mingle and move with the standard of our sister republic against the French invaders of this free continent, they will continue to move until the legions of the robber emperor are driven into their ships or into the sea.

California has asked the permission to send ten thousand troops on this side to aid our cause against the rebellion. The permission was denied. We have all the force in California, so far as men and soldiers are concerned, that can be necessary in giving sufficient aid to Mexico; but we want a fleet upon our coast; we want harbor defence; but, above all, we want the requisite arms and munitions of war. We have all the force requisite for ourselves and Mexico; give us but the facilities and the authority to apply them. When the French shall have either left their bones in the mountain passes of Mexico or taken to the sea at Vera Cruz and Guaymas, our troops may, perhaps, do good service in Texas or elsewhere where the Union cause needs soldiers.

No European Power can be strong on this continent. Our experience in 1776, and again in 1812, is full proof of this; the French embarrassments in Mexico, thus far, prove this. Four thousand miles of sea is a barrier not easily overcome. The transportation of men is one thing, the transportation of material and supplies another. France has undertaken a task greater, I think, than the estimate. It is not certain but that Mexico may herself be equal to her necessities; but I do not doubt that we can give all requisite aid without one half the sacrifice of life incurred in any one of several of the battles of the rebellion.

Some gentlemen may be timid because our commerce will suffer. So it will suffer; and so will French commerce suffer; and so has our commerce suffered before, and so must it suffer again, whenever we engage in war with a maritime State. This will be no war for a punctilio; it will be for the maintenance of an essential principle; and if it involves the lying up of our entire commercial marine, it will prove but a small sacrifice if the right be maintained. We must not sacrifice to our fears or to our love of thrift either great principles or our nation's honor. But, in fact, we are infinitely stronger upon the sea than ever before; but why not start out, as of old, our volunteer Navy, unchain our old sea lions, and set them on the track of the enemy? French commerce will be scarce upon the seas in a brief time. French looms will need cotton more than they do now. We have in every port ships, and sailors to man them; true sailors are all sea-soldiers. He who has battled fearlessly with the tempest fears no human enemy; and our sailors are the first sea-warriors of the world. France must carry on her land war upon our own continent; and we can drive her from the seas. I ask, then, what is there to fear in war with France? Not half so much as from the preservation of a treacherous peace.

It is said a war with France will give aid and comfort to the South. I would state the question differently: will it weaken this Government in its efforts to overcome this rebellion; or will it impair the chances of our ultimate success? However some of the South might be comforted by the immediate fact, it is perfectly clear, in my mind, that the war would lend strength to the Government, and essentially promote its complete re-establishment. In my judgment, a war with France would have a most healthy influence in that very direction. Its influence certainly would be to unite firmly the people of all the loyal States, and renew that war spirit that seems to have faded before military management and congressional legislation; and observe, sir, this is at this time a consummation most devoutly to be wished.

There is another consideration. How would the truly democratic masses of the South care to band with the Emperor of the French against the United States? I am of the opinion that it would greatly impair, not aid, the home strength of the rebellion. Independent of this, however, publish the full facts of the outrage of France upon Mexico; publish this to the American people. Expose the fraud, outrage and robbery being now committed by France in Mexico. Show what are the designs of France upon us. Let France appear confederating with the South. We will require no more drafting. We will need no borrowed enthusiasm. We will be stronger against the rebellion with its allies than against the rebellion as it is.

And permit me to express the opinion that this assault on free institutions by the French Emperor will detach from the rebellion many true republicans, who from this, taking warning, will seek the old standard and with us once more join hand in hand in the maintenance of the cause of free institutions.

In fine, Mr. President, I am well assured that we have nothing of value to lose by a French war. We have everything to gain, and for one I am unwilling to avoid it.

There is another subject upon which I should remark. One of the resolutions requests the President to communicate these views to the Mexican Government. If we entertain them, why should they not be expressed to the Government of Mexico? That would give them some moral aid, if nothing more; and then, why should we not make a treaty with Mexico? In the first place, I would have a reciprocity treaty with Mexico, and then there would be no question raised by Secretary Stanton or by Secretary Chase as to whether we might transact commercial exchanges generally between us and the Government of Mexico. The truth is, a reciprocity treaty would be of infinite service to Mexico, while it would be of yet greater service to ourselves. So far as I am concerned, I believe it is our duty to lend to Mexico whatever aid she may require; not denying to her the privilege of buying our old muskets, while giving to France the opportunity of buying transportation. I believe it is our duty to lend her whatever aid may be necessary; that we should spare her twenty thousand men, armed and equipped for war, or whatever number might be required.

Why, sir, the present war is not felt in the great North, except in individual families. Last fall, when I traveled in the North and West, I went through towns and villages and counties where there was no sign of war. It was only upon the great highways that you observed it. The pressure of this war is not felt; you may say it is scarcely known, except through the public press, in the States on the Pacific. We can afford to do this for Mexico. It is our duty to do all this; and I say it is of the first importance that we should assert our right and discharge our duty; and in this, we make ourselves a stronger people.

I am one of those who think that our policy in the Trent case weakened the moral power of this Government. If it were right that these commissioners should be surrendered, they should have been surrendered by terms stipulated and agreed upon between the representatives of the two Governments, so that Great Britain might have been at least committed to a rule of international law. The surrender was made as if we feared the shake of Earl Russell's head; they were surrendered in the face of a demand in the form of a threat. Nations have as much strength in their appearance of strength as they have in their armed legions.

I would have in this business the exhibition of something like national spirit, pluck, if you please. France knows what our rights are, what our wrongs have been; let her understand that we not only know them, but dare state them; (singular again, I repeat, this does not appear to have been done.) Being stated well, let our rights be firmly demanded. Is not this Government equal to this dignified duty? If France hesitates to acquiesce in our just demands, advise France that we espouse the cause of Mexico. If this be done, and properly done, I dare prophecy that the diplomatic tune of the Emperor will be played upon a different instrument, and that he will be content to dismiss for the present from his mind great visions of ambition, and trust to their realization at some more propitious season. If France persists, then let war come; this is certain, we will have done something to secure a decent respect from the other nations of the world.

I fear our Secretary regards Prince Talleyrand a proper pattern for a republican diplomatist, and admires that skill by which words may be used to conceal our thoughts, and that, in a too great effort to imitate his example, he has failed to say anything; therefore, perchance, nothing has been said. For my part, I think the sum of the science of American diplomacy may be found stated in the instructions of General Jackson to Mr. McCauley when he sent him to Tripoli. McCauley protested against the appointment, as he knew nothing about the business; and if he must go, he must have his instructions. The President replied, " your instructions will be brief, sir. *Ask for nothing but what is right, and submit to nothing that is wrong.*" The instructions proved sufficient: he continued in the discharge of his duties in Egypt until the time of his death. I wish the Government would open a school of diplomacy, and have the instructions culminate in the understanding and meaning of the Jacksonian rule and full training in the manner of its practice.

Let us demand all our rights; let us discharge all our duties. This nation will never die as long as she dares fearlessly to discharge the duties charged upon her, as long as she dares firmly and with a true faith raise erect whatever be the burden with which she may be charged. If we play the hare among animals we will be killed by the wind of the first arrow. Resistance and will and consciousness of power are the elements of strength; thus far we have been as weak as water. I have raised the question whether this shall continue. I have presented a series of resolutions, the justice and truthfulness of which cannot be disputed. Now, I desire your voices, Senators. Shall we advise tame submission, or shall we advise the assertion of ourselves as a live nation? I trust at least a direct vote may be had on the subject. I do not wish to see it buried by the legerdemain of legislation.

Established 1837.

Murphy's General Printing & Publishing Establishment,

BOOK, PAPER AND STATIONERY STORE,

Marble Building, 182 Baltimore street, Baltimore.

MEDALS *awarded* by the *Maryland Institute*, for *Printing, Book-binding* and *Bank Checks*. By the *Metropolitan Institute*, Washington, a DIPLOMA for *superior Blank Books*.

MURPHY & CO.

Booksellers, Publishers, Printers & Stationers,

WHOLESALE and RETAIL DEALERS IN

Books, Paper, Blank Books, Stationery, &c.

Constantly on hand, a large and well selected stock of

BOOKS IN GENERAL LITERATURE,

School, Classical, Miscellaneous and *Juvenile Books, &c.*

FOREIGN BOOKS: a large and varied stock, to which constant additions are made by direct importation. *Foreign Books* imported to order.

Blank Books, Paper, Stationery, &c.

Comprising a large assortment of *English, French,* and *American Letter, Cap* and *Note Papers, Envelopes, Inks, Gold and Steel Pens, Copying Presses, Copying Books, &c. &c.*, of the best qualities.

BLANK BOOKS, of every Description, made to Order, in superior styles.

BLANK BOOKS, with PRINTED HEADINGS, &c.

Made to order to any style, or pattern of Ruling, in a superior manner, at the shortest notice. Long experience, and unsurpassed facilities, in having this class of work *Printed, Ruled, Paged and Bound*, on THE PREMISES, enable us to execute all orders in this line in a very superior style, at *remarkably low rates*.

MURPHY'S UNALTERABLE STEREOGRAPHIC, and PLAIN BANK CHECKS,

In every variety; PROMISSORY NOTES, DRAFTS, BILLS OF EXCHANGE, BILLS OF LADING, BLANK DEEDS, COMMERCIAL and LAW BLANKS, &c. *kept constantly on hand*, or *Printed to order*.

PRINT TO ORDER at short notice:
Cards
Circulars
Bill-Heads
Drafts
Promissory Notes
Bank Checks
Bills Exchange
Blank Deeds
Cashiers' Blanks
Bills of Lading
Law Blanks
Law Briefs
Books
Pamphlets
Catalogues, &c.

☞ *They take pleasure in announcing that they have completed their arrangements, by which they are now enabled to keep constantly on hand a large and choice assortment of everything required in connection with the* BOOK AND STATIONERY BUSINESS. *They deem it unnecessary to enlarge on the advantages, convenience, and saving of time and expense, which this combination and concentration of stock affords to Booksellers, Colleges, Schools, Libraries, &c. &c., in being able to purchase everything at one place, at the very Lowest Rates, Wholesale and Retail.*

Plain & Ornamental Book & Job Printing,

BOOKBINDING and RULING,

Of every description, executed in the very best manner, at the lowest rates.

Having united with their Bookstore, in the same building, an extensive PRINTING OFFICE and BOOKBINDERY, well supplied with the most approved materials and experienced workmen, enable them to offer superior advantages and inducements for the *prompt, careful* and *correct execution* of every description of *Book and Job Printing, Book-Binding and Ruling*, well worthy the attention of all who may require anything in this line. ☞Particular attention paid to FINE WORK for *Banking* and other Institutions, *Insurance, Railroad, Steamboat, Transportation*, and other Joint Stock Companies, *Public Offices, &c.*

Keep constantly on hand and make to order:
Ledgers
Journals
Day Books
Cash Books
Sales Books
Blotters
Check Books
Copying Books
Bill Books
Receipt Books
Pass Books
Pocket Ledgers
Hotel Registers
Copy Books
Dockets, &c.

RAIL ROAD & COMMERCIAL PRINTING.

For nearly twenty years *Rail Road and Commercial Printing* have constituted an important branch of our business. Our experience, combined with extensive facilities, consisting of the *most approved* MACHINERY, *large fonts of* TYPE, of the latest and most approved styles; BORDERS, ENGRAVINGS, ORNAMENTS, &c. especially adapted for RAIL ROAD and COMMERCIAL WORK; also, large fonts of *Figures*, of all sizes, suitable for FREIGHT and PASSENGER TARIFFS, TABULAR WORK, &c. &c., and keeping constantly on hand a large stock of CARD BOARDS and PAPERS, of all classes, enable us to offer unsurpassed facilities for the *Prompt, Cheap* and *Correct* execution of every description of *Rail Road* and *Commercial Printing, &c.* ☞The most careful and prompt attention given to orders. Estimates and specimens furnished on application.

JOHN MURPHY & CO.

www.ingramcontent.com/pod-product-compliance
Lightning Source LLC
LaVergne TN
LVHW011132110826
845150LV00008B/2299

* 9 7 8 1 4 1 8 1 9 4 1 0 9 *